REFLECTIONS ON MY JOURNEY

NewSouth Books
105 S. Court Street
Montgomery, AL 36104

ISBN 978-1-58838-480-5

Printed in the United States of America

NEWSOUTH BOOKS • MONTGOMERY, ALABAMA
*The Black Belt, defined by its dark, rich soil, stretches
across central Alabama. It was the heart of the
cotton belt. It was and is a place of great beauty, of
extreme wealth and grinding poverty, of pain and
joy. Here we take our stand, listening to the past,
looking to the future.*

REFLECTIONS ON
MY JOURNEY

Reflections on
My Journey

I have often been asked this question: You grew up on a sharecropper farm in rural Mississippi. How did you end up on the right side of history in regard to race relations?

Let me try to answer.

My father, William Alexander Noble, was born November 22, 1865, the year the Civil War ended. The South remained occupied by Federal troops during Reconstruction, until 1877, when he was twelve. These were unbelievable, difficult years.

I was born in 1921. That was forty-four years after Reconstruction officially ended. The remaining effect of the Civil War and

Reconstruction in most of the South was the emergence of sharecropping. It was a system whereby injustice to black people was easily inflicted. Under sharecropping, the landowner furnished basic food supplies and the sharecropper could use part of the land for a vegetable garden. When the crop was harvested and sold on the market, any profit beyond the cost of furnished supplies would be shared by the landowner and the sharecropper. If the landowner was dishonest, the sharecropper would not get his or her rightful share. The sharecropper was at the mercy of the landowner. This was the situation in rural Mississippi, where I was born and grew up.

Many of my earlier memories are of the black people on our farm. In retrospect I remember three who were born in the last days of slavery and were living through the early years of the sharecropper system. One was an elderly woman we called "Aunt Girt." She patched the overalls of her mate or son, Emmett, until no part of the original overalls could be seen—all patches!

Pean Butler was an elderly black man, born in slavery, who had worked many years as a sharecropper but had gotten old and beyond working. Now and then he came to our back door to ask for something to eat. Numerous others that I did not know, if they were older than my father, were most likely born slaves, worked during Reconstruction, and were a part of the sharecropper system. Until I began thinking over my many years, I did not fully realize that my life reached so far back, so close to slavery, the devastating effects of the Civil War, and the severe years of Reconstruction. So severe was Reconstruction in the rural South, that my father received only a sixth- or eighth-grade education. Blacks often had no schooling at all.

The situation for the landowner was a step up from the sharecropper. Usually the owner would go to the bank in early spring and borrow enough money to "make a crop." The expenses for the seed, fertilizer, and machinery were paid from this loan as well as the cost of "furnishing" the sharecroppers basic food, supplies, etc. When the cotton was picked and taken to the gin, the bales of cotton would be returned to the owner's farm or house. When they were sold, then the bank loan would be paid off. One year, a "bad crop year," my father did not sell enough cotton to fully repay his loan. I remember vividly the day he returned from the bank in Utica, Mississippi, from which he had received loans for several years but which now would not loan him money for the next year. It was a terrible shock for him. Although he was able to eventually get a loan from a Raymond, Mississippi, bank, it was a hard time for my father.

My EARLY DAYS ON a sharecropper farm were

filled with much contact with black people. My brother, William, one year older than me, and I were the only two of my father's nine children that remained on the farm. During the summers we enjoyed going barefooted, but the many roots from the large oak trees in our lawn often "stumped" our toes. All but one other sibling, three half-brothers and three half-sisters, had grown up and were out of college. Our youngest brother, who was ten months old when our mother died, was being raised by an aunt in Natchez, Mississippi.

Our friends were the children of the black sharecroppers and three white boys at Learned, a small town of fewer than one hundred people. We lived three miles out in the country from Learned. One of my early memories was my feeling for our black friends that they would never have the opportunities in life that we would.

During my teenage years, William and I spent many days hoeing cotton along with the black women sharecroppers, who were paid fifty cents a day. Cotton was our main crop. Our father did not want us to stay out in the hot sun too long, so we would pause work about 11 a.m. and "cool down" under the shade trees. The memory is vivid of the breeze blowing on our shirts, wet with perspiration. We stopped for the day about 4 p.m., but the sharecroppers worked on until sundown; they had an hour off for lunch. The sharecropper men plowed the fields.

William and I had looked forward to the time we would be permitted to plow. I plowed with the horse named Minny, which I called mine, and William had his horse, Batten. On the weekends we would ride and race them, much to our pleasure.

For the first to eighth grade, we were picked up by a "school car" and taken to a three-room schoolhouse. If the black children had any school to go to, I did not know of it. There was a crossroad about two miles from our house called "Morning Star," where there was a Baptist church and a filling station. There might have been a school for the black children in the Baptist church, but any children attending would have to walk to the school. I remember realizing that something was wrong with the education system.

For the grades nine to twelve, we white children were bussed to and from Raymond, about ten miles from Learned.

At that time I was not aware of it, but in retrospect I realize that in our home we had few reading materials. There was the daily newspaper from Jackson, but I do not remember that we had many books or magazines.

I GRADUATED FROM HIGH school in 1939 and entered King College in Bristol, Tennessee, in the fall of 1939. It was the only Presbyterian college I could afford to attend and that was with a work scholarship, a small church-loan scholarship and help from a few family members.

In addition to King, there were two girl's colleges in Bristol: Sullin's and Virginia Intermont. There were no black students in any of them. I do not recall any course at King that dealt with social issues such as race relations. While there I attended the First and Central Presbyterian churches. Neither of them had any black members or blacks attending.

During these days I was aware of the racial situation, but like almost all whites, I generally accepted it as "the way it was." I didn't think about or question why that was—it just was. Nothing really occurred to me that caused me to wrestle with the wrongs of a segregated society.

However, my studies in Christianity gradually began to raise questions. It was during World War II that I entered Columbia Theological Seminary in the fall of 1942. Here the deeper study of the Christian faith and my

awareness of the larger church and the example
of ministers like Dr. McDowell Richards,
president of Columbia, and Dr. Stuart Oglesby,
long-time pastor of Central Presbyterian church
in Atlanta, helped me grow in many areas, in-
cluding race relations. I was fortunate to be the
student pastor at Central Presbyterian Church
my senior year at Seminary. Central had strong
social outreach ministry to the less fortunate
in the community. This experience raised my
awareness about social issues and I grew greatly
in many ways. I had grown up in the Lebanon
Presbyterian Church of Learned, where there
were only fifty members, so it was an education
in itself to see the effective working of a major
church such as Central.

MY FIRST PASTORATE (1945–1947) was in
McDonough, Georgia, at a small church of
seventy-five to one hundred members. Nothing
special happened there, except one small event

that sticks in my mind. I was teaching Sunday School one morning and we must have been talking about race and the way we treat people. A lawyer said if you put all people in one jar and shook it, the little ones would go to the bottom. In retrospect I wish I had been sharp enough to say that what color they are would not have determined which ones went to the bottom. That small incident shows the change that had been taking place in me.

Several years later as pastor (1947–1956) of the Second Presbyterian Church in Greenville, South Carolina, I was elected commissioner to the General Assembly of the Presbyterian Church US to its 1954 meeting in Richmond, Virginia. That year the Presbyterian Church US voted approval of the Supreme Court decision in *Brown v. Board of Education*, ending segregation in schools. At Second Church, while reporting about the General Assembly meeting I had attended, I said I was pleased that the denomination had taken the action to approve what the US Supreme Court had done. A deacon got up, walked to the back door of the sanctuary, loudly slammed the door and walked out. His action foreshadowed the coming struggle in the white churches to keep blacks from attending.

IN 1956, I WAS called by the First Presbyterian Church of Anniston, Alabama, to be their minister. After a couple of months, I went to the city hall to register to vote. I was graciously accepted but noticed several black people seated and trying to fill out the forms. They were roughly rebuffed by the clerk who refused to give any help. One question on the form was, "Will you support the laws of the U.S. and of Alabama?" I answered, "Yes. In that order." It was states' rights time and the clerk was offended by my answer. She said, "Why did you answer that way?" I said, "Because I believe that is the right order." She said, "Would you be willing to just answer yes?" I said, "No." She said, "You may not be able to vote. We will notify you." A few days later a church elder told me that he had been asked by the state representative from Anniston, "Is the new preacher at First Presbyterian Church a communist?" The elder laughed and said, "We do not think he is." Thus my ministry began in Anniston!

Somewhere along the way the Synod of Alabama of the Presbyterian Church US elected me to be a member of the board of trustees of Stillman College, a college for blacks in Tuscaloosa, Alabama. There I sat at the table with the trustees, many of whom were black. That was the first time I had ever sat at the table to eat with blacks. I was impressed that they were well-educated, responsible, and highly intelligent. I was moving, not only with my attitude about blacks, but with my feelings and emotions

Being keenly aware of what was happening in Birmingham (Bull Connor), Selma, and other Southern towns, I began to speak to various church officers and friends in the Anniston church about the need to have a "biracial council" to have communication between the races. Miller Sproull, an elder and finance commissioner for the city, indicated he was going to get such a committee appointed.

Soon thereafter I was visited by a black Baptist minister, Nimrod Reynolds, and a black Methodist minister, Bob McClain. This pivotal meeting was quite an emotional experience for all of us. Bob later recalled it in these words:

> I remember you saying, 'Brothers, let's have a word of prayer.' And you prayed like I had never heard a Southern white man pray and you cried as you prayed and I had never seen a Southern white man cry about anything that related to black people and justice. Nimrod

and I cried too. And we moved from there. That is where the movement for change in Anniston came from. Nimrod and I left the First Presbyterian Church convinced that we had met one white Christian and our hopes were renewed.

I knew that something had to be done and I was willing to do what I could. But Nimrod and Bob were the catalysts that prompted me into action.

ALL THAT I HAVE described tells how and why I was willing to serve as chair of Anniston's Biracial Human Relations Council and risk my life for what I had come to know without a doubt was right. This experience of involvement in the civil rights movement in Anniston has given a whole new dimension to my ministry, for which I am so grateful.

My book, *Beyond the Burning Bus: The Civil*

Rights Revolution in a Southern Town, tells the story of the work of the Human Relations Council in Anniston in the 1960's, which led to integration and avoidance of the major violence that occurred in many other Southern cities.

Bull Connor, police commissioner of Birmingham, Alabama, attacked civil rights workers, even children, with water hoses and dogs. Fred Shuttlesworth was an extremely brave black minister from Birmingham who experienced bombings and much harassment.

But history speaks.

Where is the name of Bull Connor to be found? Nowhere but the pages of books describing shameful things and acts.

Where is the name of Fred Shuttlesworth to be found? On the facade of the Birmingham-Shuttlesworth International Airport, named in honor of his life and courage.

About the Author

The Reverend J. Phillips Noble was born
August 18, 1921, and grew up in Learned,
Mississippi. After graduating from King
College in Bristol, Tennessee, and Columbia
Theological Seminary in Decatur, Georgia,
he was ordained a Presbyterian minister. He
completed graduate work in Edinburgh,
Scotland, and Cambridge University in
England.

From 1956 to 1971, he was pastor of

the First Presbyterian Church in Anniston, Alabama. Over his career, he also served pastorates in Georgia and South Carolina, the last of which was Charleston's historic First (Scots) Presbyterian Church. Noble was also executive secretary of the Board of Annuities and Relief and co-president of the Board of Pensions of the Presbyterian Church. He has traveled extensively on six continents. Noble was married for sixty-seven years to Betty Pope Scott, who died in 2012. They had three children (Betty, Phil Jr., and Scott) and two grandchildren.

Noble is long retired and lives now in Decatur, Georgia. On August 18, 2021, he turned one hundred years old, still alert, inquisitive, and in touch with a wide circle of family and friends.

www.ingramcontent.com/pod-product-compliance
Lightning Source LLC
Chambersburg PA
CBHW021340290326
41933CB00038B/998